THE NAUGHTY FAIRY'S
Naughtiest Ever Stories

Nick Ward

meadowside
CHILDREN'S BOOKS

The Naughtiest Fairy's Naughty Surprise
First published in 2006

The Naughtiest Ever Fairy
First published in 2004

The Naughtist Fairy's Naughty New Friend
First published in 2005

The Nicest Naughtiest Fairy
First published in 2006

This edition, first published in 2007
by Meadowside Children's Books
185 Fleet Street, London, EC4A 2HS
www.meadowsidebooks.com

All Text and illustrations © Nick Ward

The right of Nick Ward to be identified as the
author and illustrator of this work has been
asserted by him in accordance with the Copyright,
Designs and Patents Act, 1988

A CIP catalogue record for this book
is available from the British Library
Printed in Spain

10 9 8 7 6 5 4 3 2

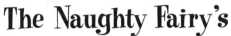

The Naughty Fairy's

NAUGHTY
SURPRISE

Nick Ward

In a quiet corner of the palace gardens, deep in a still

green pond, a little tadpole popped out of his egg...

POP!

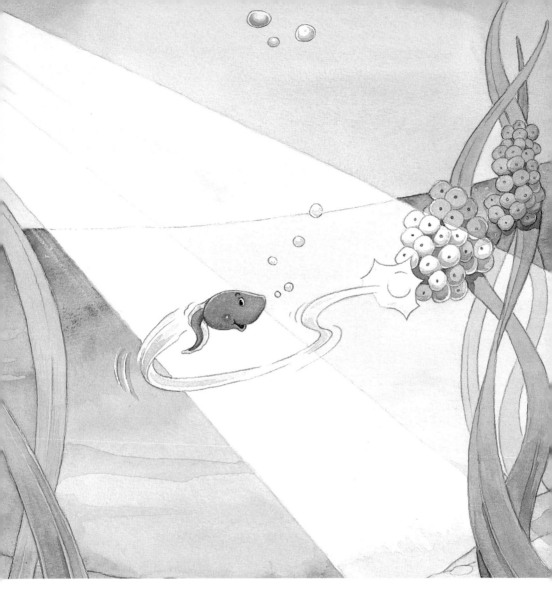

"Wow!" he gasped as he saw all the wonderful

creatures swimming around him.

"What will I be when I grow up?"

"What will I be when I grow up?" he asked a wise old fish.

"Will I be as big and brave as you?"

"What's the hurry?" smiled the wise old fish.

"Anything may happen. Just wait and see!"

So the impatient little tadpole waited ...

and waited ...

until one day...

"Well, who would have guessed!"

croaked the little frog, jumping onto a lily-pad.

"I'm a fr-"

But just then a passing princess scooped him up.

"Are you my handsome prince?" she asked, giving him a kiss.

"Oh dear," said the frog, feeling another change coming on...

"I'm a handsome prince!" he cried,

and was just about to give the Princess another kiss, when...

WHOOOSH!

A naughty fairy grabbed the Princess

and whisked her away to a tall rickety tower.

"**HELP!**" she cried. "Save me!"

So the Handsome Prince ran through the woods

and over a mountain, till he came to the tall rickety tower.

But two ugly trolls were guarding the tower.

"Gnarr!" they roared, scrunching up their faces.

"That's not scary," said the Handsome Prince.

And he pulled such horrible faces that the trolls screamed

and ran away! So the Handsome Prince rescued the

Princess, which turned him into a...

Hero!

"Hero!" sighed the Princess, "You're my hero!"

So the Hero quickly marched the Big Bad Wolf and some big

bully giants out of town. (That was a hero's job, you see.)

"And don't come back till you're sorry!" he ordered.

The Princess was so grateful to him for making her country safe that she decided to marry her hero.

And this turned him into a rich and powerful...

POP!

King!

King! He was a kind and considerate king and was loved

by all his subjects, right down to the lowliest pig farmer.

They lived in a beautiful palace and were very happy.

Soon the King and Queen had a baby daughter,

and this turned the King into a...

"Daddy! Yippee, I'm a daddy!"

He was so excited that he held a huge party.

Everyone was invited:

     the Three Bears, the Three Little Pigs

         and Little Red Riding Hood.

Everyone except the Naughty Fairy!

She was so annoyed that she wrapped a naughty magic

spell in a box, and tied a beautiful bow on top.

"I'll teach him!" she grumbled.

The Naughty Fairy put on a disguise

and took her present to the King...

"Congratulations!" she cackled.

But the King recognized the Fairy

and guessed it was a trick.

"I can't undo the bow," he pretended.

"Oh, give it here, silly!" said the Naughty Fairy.

Fizz

And she ripped off the paper and opened the box.

"Oh no!"

The magic spell whizzed around the Fairy's head and

Pop! she disappeared.

"Where has she gone?" cried the King.

POP!

In a quiet corner of the palace gardens,

deep in a still green pond, a naughty little tadpole

gasped at all the wonderful creatures.

"What will I be when I grow up?"

she wondered...

The
NAUGHTIEST
ever
FAIRY

Nick Ward

High on a green hill, in a little yellow house,

lived the Naughtiest Ever Fairy. After a busy morning

thinking up tricks and mixing spells,

the Naughtiest Ever Fairy liked to take a nap.

Across the valley, in a big, blue castle, lived the very Noisy

Giant. He spent the morning hard at work with his very

noisy chores but, when his chores were done, the Very

Noisy Giant loved to dance.

Every afternoon, just as the Naughtiest Ever Fairy climbed into bed and closed her eyes, the Very Noisy Giant would put on his favourite noisy music.

CLUMP!

Then he would skip and spin in his giant boots...

It was getting harder and harder for the

Naughtiest Ever Fairy to get any sleep at all.

RATTLE!
CLATTER!
CRASH!

The Naughty Fairy woke with a jump.

She had had enough.

She couldn't get her beauty sleep

and it was starting to show.

As you can imagine,

the Naughty Fairy was

getting very grumpy!

"If the giant wasn't so BIG," she thought,

"he wouldn't make so much NOISE!"

And that gave the Fairy a naughty idea.

Soon it would be the giant's birthday,

so the Fairy sat down to make a special card

and inside she wrote a very naughty spell...

...in fact, the spell was so naughty that I can't tell you what it said until the magic has worn off!

"That should do the trick," smiled the Naughty Fairy, and she popped it in the post-box.

On his birthday, a card popped through the letter-box.

"Yippee!" he cried. "Who's it from?"

"Oh no!" said the Giant. "I forgot. I can't read!"

So he went to find someone very clever who could read.

"Can you read my card?" he asked the Big Bad Wolf.

"Of course," growled the Wolf importantly,

as he grabbed the card from the Giant's hand.

"I'm a very good reader!"

"What does it say?" asked the Giant.

"Hold on, I've got to read it to myself first," growled the Big Bad Wolf. And suddenly Kazam!

The Big, Bad Wolf changed...

And he ran away to hide.

The Noisy Giant still didn't know what his card said,

so he went to see...

roar!

...the Bold and Roaring Lion
(who was king of the jungle).

"Can you read my card?" asked the Very Noisy Giant.

"Of course," roared the Lion imperiously.

"I'm a very good reader!"

He opened the card and started to read.

KaZam! The Lion changed...

...into a little scaredy-cat!

"Oh, how humiliating!"

he meowed,

running off to hide.

"I'm supposed to be the king of the jungle!"

But still the Noisy Giant didn't know

what his card said, so he went to see...

...the Last of the Fiery Dragons.

"Can you read my card?"

asked the Giant.

"Of course," said the Dragon. "I'm a very good reader!"

But as soon as he started to read the message,

Kazam! The Fiery Dragon changed...

...into an insignificant little worm!

"Oh, this is insufferable!" squirmed the Worm,

crawling into his tiny hole.

"I'm supposed to be a fiery dragon!"

The poor Giant still didn't know what his card said,

so he went to see...

...the Naughtiest Ever Fairy.

"Giant!" she gasped, very surprised to see him still

so big and noisy. "Didn't you get your card?"

"Yes," said the Giant. "But I can't read it. Can you help?"

"No chance," said the Fairy.

"I'm not falling

for that old trick.

Find someone else to read it for you..."

Whoever reads this
birthday card,
If you're big or fierce
or scary,
Will turn into something
very small,
love from the
Naughty Fairy.

Kazam!

(Oh you didn't,
did you?)

The Naughtiest Fairy's

NAUGHTY
NEW FRIEND

Nick Ward

The Naughtiest Ever Fairy sat at her

kitchen table and sulked.

"I want someone to play with," she said.

"Someone naughty and fun - just like me!"

And then she had an idea...

Two frogs, one snail,
some stinky garlic,
And a lizard's tail.

she sang, mixing the
ingredients into a bowl.

Salt for fun,
and a pinch of pepper
for naughtiness...

Extra
Sneezy
Pepper

Eyes!

If she wanted a friend, she could make one!

(She was a fairy, after all.)

"Brilliant!" she cried, flicking through her book of spells.

"Whoops!" she cried, as she knocked the whole bag of

pepper into her bowl. "Oh never mind."

She waved her magic wand over the mixture.

There stood the Naughty

Fairy's new friend...

"Excellent!"

another naughty fairy

- just like her!

The New Naughty

Fairy cheered

"Fantastic!"

"Let's have

some fun!"

The two friends went straight
to the giant's castle.

The Giant was stomping about in
his heavy gardening boots,
watering his flowers.

"He's much too noisy," said the Naughty Fairy.

"Watch this."

She waved her magic wand, and...

The Giant started to inflate

like a huge balloon.

"What's happening?"

he cried as he floated, light as a feather, across the valley.

"Get me down!"

"Hee, hee," laughed the fairies and away they flew.

"I can be much naughtier than that," said the New Naughty Fairy as they flew past the village school.

" AND THE MOST FEARSOME DINOSAUR OF ALL," SHE SAID, "WAS... "

The two fairies peered through the window where old Miss Munchet was reading to her class.

(The New Naughty Fairy waved her wand.)

"... the TEACHERSAURUS REX!" she roared, crashing her huge jaws together.

"Help," cried the children as the Teachersaurus Rex chased them out into the playground.

"That was brilliant," laughed the New Naughty Fairy

when they got home. "I'm the naughtiest fairy ever."

"No, I'm the naughtiest fairy ever," said the Naughty Fairy.

"No, you're the silliest fairy ever!"

"Oh yeah?" said the Naughty Fairy, stamping her foot,

"I'm not playing with you anymore."

"Then I'll make a new friend," said the New Naughty Fairy,

grabbing the Naughty Fairy's bowl of magic mix.

She rushed outside.

"Watch this," she cried, waving her magic wand...

POP! There was another naughty fairy.

And that naughty fairy said,

"I want a new friend."

POP! ... and that naughty fairy
made a new friend, POP!
until... POP! POP! POP!

"This," said the Naughty Fairy, "is the result of too much pepper. STOP!"

But the fairies kept on appearing;

and each new fairy was being

very, very naughty.

They made the grass turn blue and the sky green;

hills wobbled like jelly and the clouds rained ink;

rats as big as cats chased dogs that hopped like frogs!

Soon, everything was in a terrible muddle!

"Stop!" yelled the Naughty Fairy.

(Enough, after all, is enough!)

But each time she made one fairy disappear, a new fairy
materialized. "How on earth am I going to stop them?"

she cried, when...

"Watch out below!" called the Giant,

falling from the sky as the spell wore off. **CRASH!**

The Giant landed in a cloud of pink, peppery, magic dust.

Kazam!

All the naughty fairies disappeared...

...all except the Naughtiest Ever Fairy.

"Well done, Giant," she gasped.

"You're a hero."

Atchoo!

"Oh, it was nothing," sneezed the Giant

through a fog of pepper dust. "Atchoo!"

"Now I think I can take a well earned rest,"

sighed the Naughty Fairy, making her way indoors.

The
NICEST
NAUGHTIEST
FAIRY

Nick Ward

"Oh good!" thought the Naughtiest Ever Fairy, as a letter popped through her letterbox.

Dear Naughty Fairy,

STOP being so naughty! We've had enough of being turned into toads and trolls and wobbly jellies. If you don't stop your naughty tricks we will drum you out of town!

Lots of love from your friends,

It was a letter from all of her neighbours,

and it wasn't a very nice one either...

"Oops," thought the Naughtiest Ever Fairy.

She didn't fancy being drummed out of town, so she decided

to be a well-behaved little fairy. Starting straight away!

The Very Noisy Giant was busy crashing about, spring-cleaning his castle when the Well-behaved Naughty Fairy arrived.

GRANNY GIANT.

"I can help you with that," she shouted above the din.

"No!" cried the Noisy Giant.

"I know your naughty tricks."

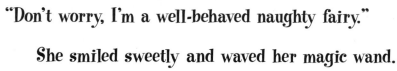

"Don't worry, I'm a well-behaved naughty fairy."

She smiled sweetly and waved her magic wand.

But although the Naughty Fairy tried to be good,

her magic was determined to be especially naughty,

and almost at once things started to go wrong...

Paintbrushes whizzed through the air, sloshing paint over the walls, the windows and the Giant as well!

The vacuum sucked up the rubbish,

the rugs and just about

everything else!

"Sorry," said the Good Naughty Fairy

and quickly flew off to help somebody else.

The Big Bad Wolf
was trying to
huff and puff
a house down.

"Oh, please let me help," volunteered the Good Naughty

Fairy, and summoned up a wind so strong it blew the

Wolf's clothes right off and sent the house spinning across

the valley and far out to sea...

"HELP!" shouted the Three Little Pigs, still in the house.

"Don't worry, I'm coming," cried the Naughty Fairy.

But on the way, she met someone else who needed help...

The Boiled

Sweet Maker

lived at the top

of a steep hill

and he was mixing

a huge pot of sweet smelling candy,

when the Naughty Fairy passed by.

"Don't interrupt me now,"
puffed the Candy Man.

"I have to finish
all the sweets for
the Mayor's very
important procession."

"Oh, let me help," cried the Well-behaved Naughty Fairy.
And before the sweet maker could shout 'No!' she had
waved her magic wand.

KAZAM!

The pot began to rattle and shake, and WOOSH! the gooey mixture erupted out of the pot, spilling across the floor.

"Stop it!" cried the Sweet Maker as the sticky mess bubbled out of the door and down the hill.

But the Well-behaved Naughty Fairy had already gone.

All the way down the hill, townsfolk were getting stuck in the mucky mess.

The Mayor's important procession had been brought to a standstill, up to their knees in toffee.

"I might have known it was you," yelled the Mayor, shaking his fist as the Naughty Fairy flew by.

Soon the Naughty Fairy came upon the Bold and
Roaring Lion (who was King of the Jungle).
He was having a royal nap.

"Ah, he's sleeping like a baby," said the Helpful Fairy.

"I'll just make him a little more comfortable."

She waved her magic wand and...

The Mighty King of the Jungle awoke to find himself

dressed in a baby's bonnet and nappy, rocking in a cradle!

"How embarrassing," he roared. "Just you wait!"

But by now the Naughty Fairy had flown out to sea to help the Three Little Pigs, whose house was still bobbing about on the waves.

"Fairy to the rescue!" she cried, waving her magic wand...

KAZAM!

A huge and hungry whale arched out of the sea and gobbled up the Pigs and their house in one mouthful!

Up through the clouds it swam, turning and somersaulting and emitting polite little burps. (A house is a big meal after all, even for an enormous whale!)

"Come back," called the Good Naughty Fairy, waving her magic wand...

The Whale belly-flopped into the village pond.

("Oof," gasped the whale as the Little Pig's house

shot out of his mouth).

Pond water and pond life rained
down on the town.

KASPLOSH!

Mrs Munchet,
the Schoolteacher,
was covered in slime and
weeds and frogspawn...
The Baker's magnificent
cake for the Mayor's procession
was drenched in pond water...
And the Last of the Fiery Dragon's fiery breath
was snuffed out in the downpour.

"This is one of the Naughty Fairy's tricks," they spluttered.

"Oh no!" cried the Well-behaved Naughty Fairy,

desperately waving her magic wand

as it rained frogs and newts.

POP!

But **POP!** her naughty magic turned one of the
frogs into her naughty new friend, who was delighted to
see the mess the Naughtiest Ever Fairy had made.

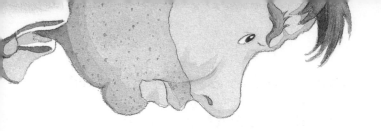

All the townspeople marched up to the

Well-behaved Naughty Fairy.

What a state! They were covered in slime and toffee and duckweed. (The Naughty Fairy couldn't help but giggle).

"Are you responsible for this shambles?" demanded the Mayor.

"It's not my fault," complained the Well-behaved Naughty Fairy. "I've been good, but my magic was naughty."

"Tidy this mess up," ordered Mrs Munchet.

"And no magic, or I'll turn you into a sausage!" added the Naughty New Friend.

Ignoring the Naughty New Friend, the Well-behaved Naughty Fairy waved her magic wand to start the big tidy up,

but...

"That's not fair," grumbled the Naughtiest Ever Sausage,

as she started the long task of mopping up.

"In future I'm going

to stay naughty...

It's safer!"

meadowside
CHILDREN'S BOOKS